Aberdeenshire

COUNCIL

Aberdeenshire Library and Information Service
www.aberdeenshire.gov.uk/libraries
Renewals Hotline 01224 661511

3 0 MAR 2012
1 1 MAY 2012

VEITCH, CATHERINE

A World of Farming

Farms Around the World

Catherine Veitch

www.raintreepublishers.co.uk
Visit our website to find out more information about Raintree books.

To order:
☎ Phone 0845 6044371
🖷 Fax +44 (0) 1865 312263
🖳 Email myorders@raintreepublishers.co.uk

Customers from outside the UK please telephone +44 1865 312262

Raintree is an imprint of Capstone Global Library Limited, a company incorporated in England and Wales having its registered office at 7 Pilgrim Street, London, EC4V 6LB – Registered company number: 6695582

Edited by Daniel Nunn, Rebecca Rissman, and Harriet Milles
Designed by Joanna Hinton-Malivoire
Picture research by Mica Brancic
Originated by Capstone Global Library Ltd.
Production by Victoria Fitzgerald
Printed and bound in China by Leo Paper Products Ltd

ISBN 978 1 406 22899 1 (hardback)
15 14 13 12 11
10 9 8 7 6 5 4 3 2 1

British Library Cataloguing in Publication Data
Veitch, Catherine.
 Farms around the world. – (Acorn plus)
 1. Farms–Pictorial works–Juvenile literature.
 2. Agriculture–Pictorial works–Juvenile literature.
 3. Farm life–Pictorial works–Juvenile literature.
 I. Title II. Series
 630-dc22
A full catalogue record for this book is available from the British Library.

Acknowledgements
We would like to thank the following for permission to reproduce photographs: Alamy **p. 19** (© D. Hurst); iStockphoto **pp. 16, 22b** (© Zmeel Photography); Shutterstock **pp. 4 left** (© Lenice Harms), **4 right** (© Emi Cristea), **5 left** (© Mircea Bezergheanu), **5 right** (© Andreas G. Karelias), **6 top left** (© Pavel Mitrofanov), **6 bottom left** (© BestPhoto1), **6 right** (© Javarman), **7 left** (© Joy M. Prescott), **7 top right** (© Pack-Shot), **7 bottom right** (© Arkady_S), **8** (© Lizette Potgieter), **9** (© Euro Color Creative), **9 inset** (© Elena Rostunova), **10, 22a** (© Evlakhov Valeriy), **10 inset, 22f** (© Rudchenko Liliia), **11** (© Sia Chen How), **11 inset** (© Elena Elisseeva), **12** (© Jakub Pavlinec), **12 inset** (© Lasse Kristensen), **13** (© Grisha), **14, 22c** (© Mats), **14 inset 22e** (8690472142), **15 left** (© Henk Bentlage), **15 right** (© Gualtiero Boffi), **16 inset, 22d** (© Smit), **17** (© Dariusz Gora), **18** (© Local Favorite Photography), **20** (© Richard Thornton), **21** (© Charles Amundson).

Front cover photograph of a rice plantation in Thailand reproduced with permission of Shutterstock (© Worakit Sirijinda). Back cover photograph of sheep being sheared reproduced with permission of Shutterstock (© Mats).

We would like to thank Patricia Wooster for her invaluable help in the preparation of this book.

Every effort has been made to contact copyright holders of any material reproduced in this book. Any omissions will be rectified in subsequent printings if notice is given to the publisher.

Contents

Some words appear in bold, **like this**. You can find out what they mean in "Words to know" on page 23.

What is a farm?

A farm is a place where animals are kept or plants are grown. Some animals are kept for food. Some animals are kept for **materials**, such as wool.

orange

flowers

Some farms grow plants. Plants can be grown for food. Some plants are grown for materials. Some plants are grown for their flowers.

Farms that grow crops

bananas

grapes

raspberry

Some farms grow **crops**. A crop is a plant that is grown on a farm. Some farms grow fruit crops. Bananas, raspberries, and grapes are fruits.

peas

carrot

potatoes

Some farms grow vegetables. A vegetable is a crop.
Peas, carrots, and potatoes are vegetables.

clothes made from cotton

cotton

Some farms grow cotton. Cotton is a **material crop**.
The fluffy white cotton grows around the seeds of the
cotton plant. Cotton can be made into clothes.

tulips

Some farms grow flowers as crops. Tulips, daffodils, and roses are flowers. The flowers are sold in shops around the world.

wheat

food made from wheat

Some farms grow **grains**. Grains are the seeds of some **crops**. Wheat is a grain. Wheat is made into flour. Bread, biscuits, pasta, and cakes are made from flour.

rice

rice plant

Rice is also a grain. Rice needs lots of water to grow. It is grown in fields flooded with water. These fields are called **paddy** fields.

Some farms grow oilseed rape. Oilseed rape is a **crop**. Oilseed rape can be used to make **fuel** for cars.

Most crops are planted in the spring. The crops need sunlight and water to grow. The crops are picked in the autumn.

Farms that keep animals

Some farms keep sheep for their wool. Farmers use a special tool to cut off the wool. Some wool is made into clothes and carpets.

lamb

shepherd

Some farms keep sheep for meat. **Lamb** and **mutton** meat come from sheep. A farmer who looks after sheep is sometimes called a **shepherd**.

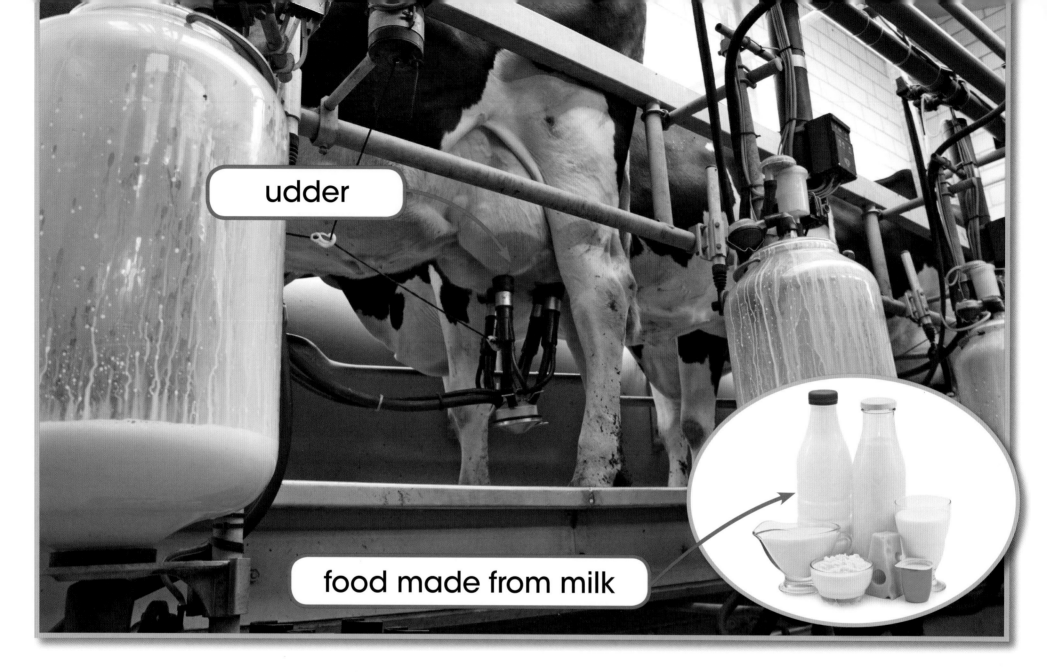

udder

food made from milk

Some farms keep cattle for their milk. The milk comes out of the cows' **udders**. Cheese, cream, yoghurt, and butter are all made from milk.

Some farms keep cattle for meat. **Beef** meat comes from cattle. Steak, mince, and burgers can all be made from beef meat.

chicken coop

Some farms keep chickens for meat. The chickens have a shelter called a **chicken coop**. The chickens are put in the coop at night. The coop protects them from animals that may hunt them for food.

18

collecting eggs

Some farms keep chickens for eggs. The farmer collects the eggs each day. Then the eggs are put in boxes. The boxes of eggs are sold in shops.

Getting food and materials from farms

Farmers sell their food and **materials**. Lorries take the food and materials from farms to shops. Some food and materials also travel by aeroplane.

We can buy farm food and materials in shops. We can buy farm food and materials at markets. What has your family bought that comes from a farm?

Can you remember?

Match up each **crop** or animal with the thing that is made from it.

Answers on page 24

Words to know

beef meat from a cow

chicken coop large cage or pen where chickens are kept

crop plant grown on a farm. Many crops are used for food.

fuel something we put into cars and lorries to make them go

grains seeds of some plants. Wheat and rice are grains.

lamb meat from a young sheep

material something that is used to make something else

mutton meat from an adult sheep

paddy field flooded with water where rice is grown

shepherd person who looks after sheep

udder bag-like part that hangs under a female animal. It is where milk comes from.

Index

Answers to quiz on page 22:
a) matches with f); b) matches with d); c) matches with e)

Notes for parents and teachers

Before reading

Show the children the front cover of the book. Guide children in a discussion about what they know about farms. Tell the children that farms are where animals are kept or plants are grown. Farmers use animals and plants for different things.

After reading

- Make a list on the whiteboard or on a large piece of paper of what the children learned. Create two columns labelled "materials" and "food". Ask each child to come up with an example of a material grown or kept on a farm, or a food grown or kept on a farm. Are they wearing any cotton or woollen clothing? What did they eat for their breakfast or lunch that may have come from a farm?